Oodles of Doodles

by
Mike Artell

STERLING PUBLISHING CO., INC.
New York

Library of Congress Cataloging-in-Publication Data available upon request.

10   9   8   7   6   5   4

Published by Sterling Publishing Company, Inc.
387 Park Avenue South, New York, NY 10016
© 2002 by Mike Artell
Distributed in Canada by Sterling Publishing
^{c}/o Canadian Manda Group, One Atlantic Avenue, Suite 105
Toronto, Ontario, Canada M6K 3E7
Distributed in Great Britain and Europe by Chris Lloyd
at Orca Book Services, Stanley House, Fleets Lane,
Poole BH15 3AJ, England.
Distributed in Australia by Capricorn Link (Australia) Pty. Ltd.
P.O. Box 704, Windsor, NSW 2756 Australia.

Sterling ISBN 0-8069-9366-9

Oodles of Drewdles for my nephew,

DREW POPE

Introduction

This book will show you how to draw great little doodles. What is a doodle? A doodle is a simple cartoon that people draw when they're talking on the phone or listening to a boring speaker. Doodles let people keep their hands busy without making their brains work too hard. The great thing about doodles is that they can really improve a person's drawing skills and the ability to think creatively. You don't have to be a great artist to be a doodler. All you need is a pencil, something to write on, and this book.

Ready to get started? Good! Call someone on the phone, start talking, and get yourself doodling!

Before you start...

If you're going to doodle, you'll need a pencil with a good eraser and something to draw on. A blank sheet of plain, white paper is always good, but you can also draw in the margins of the telephone book, on a "sticky note," or on the back of an envelope. Don't draw on something that's going to get you in trouble.

Doodle fast. Don't try to make your doodles perfect. Just for the heck of it, see how many you can draw in 60 seconds. The idea here is to keep it simple and fun.

Ready? Let's doodle!

Acorns

Draw a rainbow and add a wavy line on the bottom.

Add a small cone on top for a stem.

Now draw a smiley-face shape. Add some criss-cross lines and you've drawn an acorn!

If they get the right amount of food, water and sunlight, acorns can grow into big, strong oak trees.

Anchors

Draw this shape.

Add a "J" and a backward "J."

Draw some points on the ends of the "J's."

Underwater scenes look more realistic when you add an anchor.

Ants

Draw a head. Add an egg-shape and a circle.

Now draw a tail. Add six legs.

Just for fun, try drawing your ants little,

like this...   →

Apples

Step 1.   **Step 2.**

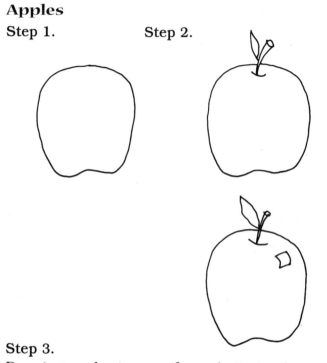

Step 3.
Drawing apples is easy if you do it step-by-step.

Apples come in lots of different shapes and sizes.
Uh-oh. Looks like somebody got hungry.

Awards

Start by drawing a rectangle. Then draw another rectangle inside of it. Add the word, "Award" then draw some squiggly lines underneath.

This guy is very proud of the award he won.

Bald

Draw the bottom half of a head.

Add some eyes and a mouth.

This guy is almost bald.

This guy is REALLY bald.

Bald

Do you know what kind of bird this is?

A BALD eagle.

Bananas

Draw a curved line and add the number 7 on each end.

Now draw a smiley-face shape.

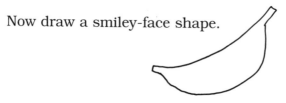

Color the ends and add some lines on the side of the banana.

If you overlap several drawings of bananas, you can draw a big banana bunch!

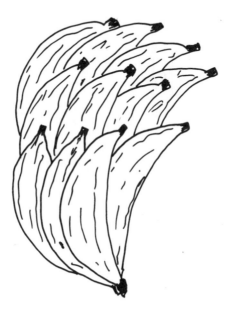

Barbells

Draw two sets of rectangles. Add two small rectangles on the ends.

Now draw two lines between the rectangles—and coming out at the ends.

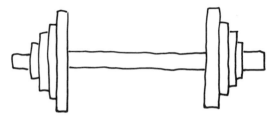

It's funny if you draw a little animal or person lifting a heavy set of barbells.

Baskets

Draw a smiley-face shape then add an oval across the top. Make a big rainbow shape for the handle. Draw 3 lines going up and down, and then draw 3 lines going sideways. Keep doing this until you cover the entire basket.

Baskets come in lots of different shapes and sizes. Try drawing some baskets that are new and different. No matter what shape you draw, you can always make your baskets look woven by adding 3 lines in each direction.

Bones

Draw a backward "3," skip a space, then draw a regular "3."

Connect those two shapes with two straight lines.

This dog likes to think about bones.

Draw your own X-ray machine. All you have to do is draw a rectangle in front of someone's body and you can show their bones. Is that cool or what?

Braces

Draw a smiley face. Show lots of teeth. Add little squares on each tooth. Connect each of the squares with a line.

Wouldn't it be funny if animals got braces on their teeth? Animals like beavers and sharks would sure look weird with braces.

Cactus

Draw a curvy line. Add two straight lines.

Now draw some "stickers" and flowers
on top.

Add some mountains and rocks and it looks like you're in the middle of the desert.

Caps

Draw the bottom part
of a face, and then add
a curvy line.

Draw a bump on top.

Add some lines on the bump
and you've drawn a cap.

Lots of guys wear their caps backwards.

Caterpillars

Draw a smiley face and add some antennae.

Add circles...

and add feet.

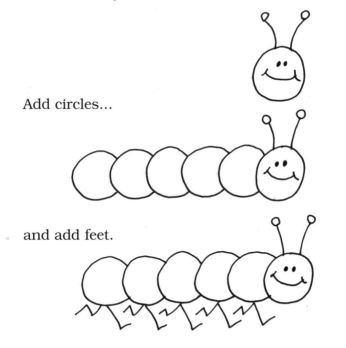

Try adding polka dots, funny feet, stingers and other special effects to your caterpillar.

Cheese

Draw a triangle.

Add sides and a bottom.

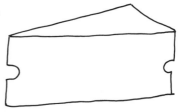

Now all we need are a few holes.

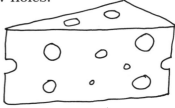

Looks like it's time for a snack.

Clouds

Draw some bumpy shapes on the top. Draw smiley face shapes on the bottom. Make the bottoms of your clouds "flatter" than the tops.

Adding some shading on the bottom side of the cloud makes it look a little more realistic.

Crying

Draw tears coming from the eyes. Turn the mouth down on the ends. Add a little wavy line under the mouth.

Whoa! This girl is REALLY crying.

Darkness

If you want it to look like it's dark outside, draw silhouettes.

If you want things to look scary, just draw the
eyes and make everything else dark.

Darts

Darts are shaped like human eyes. All you have to
add is a triangle on one end and a point on the
other end. Here are some darts on a dartboard.

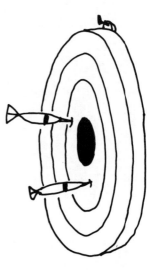

Porcupines love this game because they NEVER run out of darts.

Dawn

To draw the dawn, draw a small hill and then add a big bump for the sun.

Everyone likes the dawn, but not when it means you have to get out of a nice, warm bed.

Delicious

When something is delicious, cartoon people lick their lips. Sometimes they even drool. (yuck)

When something smells wonderful, cartoon people might even rub their tummies thinking about how good it's going to taste.

Diapers

Diapers look a little like triangles with two bumps on the top two points. Most of the time, you'll draw diapers on little kids...

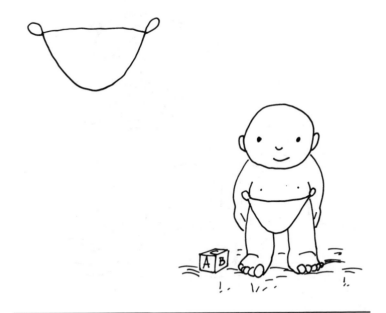

But sometimes it looks funny to draw diapers on little animals.

Doors

People usually draw doors closed like this...

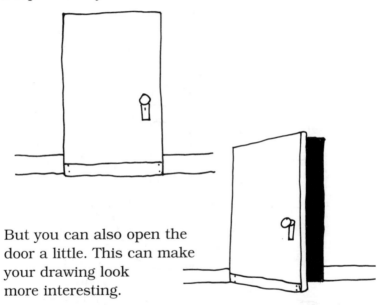

But you can also open the
door a little. This can make
your drawing look
more interesting.

If you draw a door on the floor, it becomes a secret trap door.

Earth

Draw a circle.

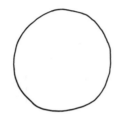

Add a north and south pole.

Draw some land on the left and right sides of the ball and it looks like the planet Earth.

Put a face on the planet Earth and let it tell us something about itself.

Eggs

Most people draw eggs as an oval shape. But here's another way to draw an egg....First draw a rainbow shape. Add a curved line on the bottom.

Now draw a curvy line that looks like this....Add a little shading and some "heat" lines and you've got a fried egg.

Some eggs are large and some eggs are small.
Here's a cartoon about some very small eggs.

Envelopes

An envelope is usually a rectangle. Here's how it looks from the front...

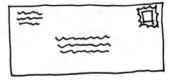

And here's how it looks from the back.

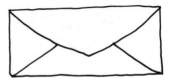

The next time you write a letter to someone, try
drawing lots of cartoons and original artwork on
the envelope.

Eyes

Here are a few kinds of eyes: pretty, simple, worried, scary, impatient, and wacky.

Try drawing a face 4 times and change the eyes each time.

Feet

Here is a foot from the side:

Here is what a foot looks like from the front:

LOOK OUT! IT'S BIGFOOT!

Fire

Fire can look like a leaf or like a crab's claw...

Leaf Crab's claw

Leaf

Leaf and crab's claw...

If you want to draw fire coming out of the back of a race car, just draw the fire sideways.

Fish

Draw an oval. Add a mouth and eyes.

Add a tail fin. Finish by adding fins on the top and bottom of the fish. Bubbles make the fish look as if it's underwater.

Just for fun, try drawing unusual-shaped bodies
for your fish.

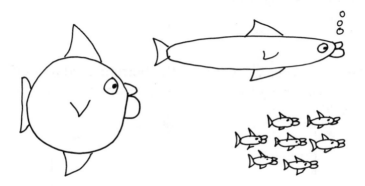

Flags

Start with a wavy line.

Add two straight lines.

Draw another wavy line at the bottom. Add a circle and two straight lines, and you've drawn a flag on a pole.

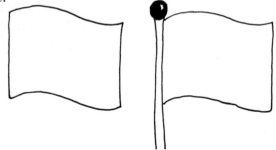

You can draw flags from different countries. If you make your flag pointed on one end, it becomes a pennant.

Flies

If you draw a dot, add two wings and some little curvy lines, you'll have drawn a fly.

Dot + 2 wings + some little curvy lines

PEE - YEW! Flies love to hang around stinky, smelly stuff.

Hmmmm...looks like somebody is about to have some "fast food" for dinner.

Frogs

Frogs start out as a smiley face with legs...

Add a body and 2 big back legs.

"Kiss me and I'll become a prince."

Ghosts

Start with a round head and two arms.

Add a body. Draw round eyes and a round mouth.

You can make your ghosts sweet. Or angry.

Or even shy.

Gingerbread Men

Start by drawing an outline of the gingerbread man. Next, add "dot" eyes, mouth, and buttons. Also, add a little shading on the edges.

Draw lots of little gingerbread men on a Christmas tree.

Glass

Draw two slanted lines on windows to make it look like glass. Like this:

Uh-oh...is someone missing a baseball? I think one just broke the glass in this window.

Gloves

Draw a shape that looks like a hand. Now draw little short lines to show where the glove is sewn.

When you work in the garden, it's a good idea to wear gloves.

Glue

To draw glue, first draw a little puddle (like water), and then draw stringy stuff. Take a look:

GRRR...

STRINGY STUFF

GLUE

Have you ever had this happen to you?

Grass

Most of the time, people draw grass straight up
and down. Everyone who thinks this is boring,
please say, "Boring!"

BORING!

Instead, try drawing some blades of grass bent to
one side. Draw some of the blades longer too.

COOL—

Some kinds of grass are long and pointy. Here's an example:

Guitars

Draw this shape.

Add a neck for your guitar.

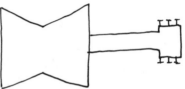

Now draw strings and knobs.

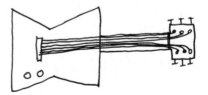

Acoustic guitars are more rounded. Here's how to draw an acoustic guitar.

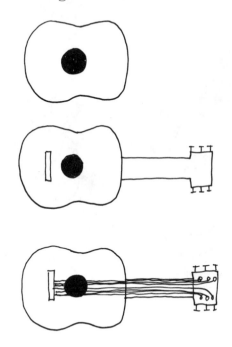

Hair

Every now and then, draw really weird hair on your cartoon characters. It's funny!

Sometimes hair is so long that it covers the cartoon character's eyes. HA!

Hammers

Draw this shape.   Add this...

Now draw a handle for your hammer.

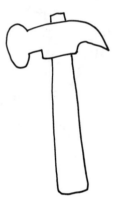

Your fingers would appreciate it if you would be very careful when you use a hammer.

Hands

Draw a circle.

Add fingers.

Erase the part of the circle
at the base of each finger
and at the wrist.

Sometimes, this is all you can see of a hand.
When someone is holding a soda can, the can
hides most of the hand.

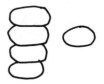

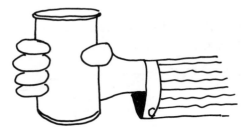

Hatchets

First, draw the blade. Next, add the top of the handle.

Add the rest of the handle and presto, you've drawn a hatchet.

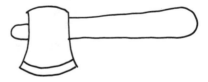

It must be Thanksgiving Day...this turkey looks very nervous.

Hearts

Draw one of these. Now draw one on the other side.

Add some "bumps" around the edge. Write the words, "I love you" in the heart.

When cartoon characters are in love, little hearts float around their heads.

Hot Dogs

Draw the top bun.

Draw the hot dog.

Draw the bottom bun. Add mustard.

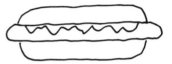

Here's another kind of "hot dog."

Ice

Draw a diamond. Draw the sides of the ice cube.

Add a "V" shape on the bottom. Draw slanted lines on the side of the ice cube.

Here are several ice cubes floating in a nice cool glass of lemonade. Mmmm.

Ideas

When cartoon characters get ideas, a light bulb appears above their heads.

Here's how to draw a light bulb in 3 steps:

1.   2.   3.

This cartoon character hasn't gotten an idea yet.
His light switch is still turned off.

Insects

To draw insects, just connect a bunch of ovals and circles. Here are some examples:

Insects have 6 legs. If you're drawing cartoon insects, remember to give them 6 legs, not 8 legs like a spider.

Irons

Draw this shape...

Add dials on top and holes on the side

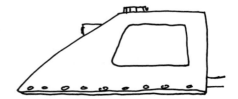

Uh-oh. It looks like somebody left the iron plugged-in. What do you think might happen?

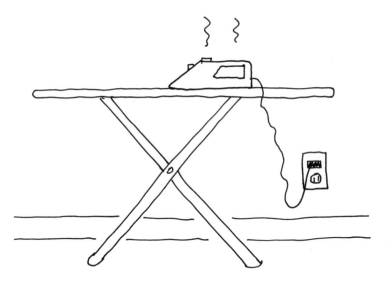

Islands

To draw an island, first draw some water.

Add a sandy bump above the water.

Now draw a simple palm tree.

This character has been stuck on this island for a long time. What could he be thinking about?

Jail

If you want to draw someone in jail, draw the person with his hands in front of him like this:

Next add bars. Make sure that the bars touch the character's hands.

It seems like this bird is not happy in its cage.

Jellyfish

Draw a big smile and two round eyes.
Draw an uneven shape all around
the mouth and eyes.

Add tentacles.

Is it possible that our jellyfish has fallen in love?

Jewels

First draw some diamonds, circles, and
hexagons...then draw a star inside of each one.

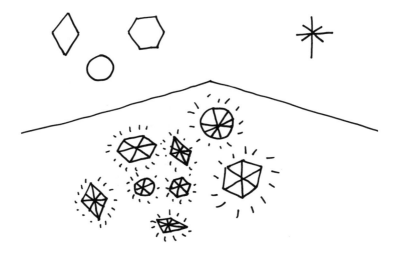

Draw jewels on cartoon characters' hands, ears and necks.

Jumping

Draw Picture 1 on a sheet of paper then draw Picture 2 on another sheet of paper.

Lay Picture 2 on top of Picture 1. Flip up and down and your cartoon character will look like he's jumping!

Kayaks

Draw a long, flat oval that's pointy on each end.

Add a hole in the top and a smiley-face shape on the bottom.

Brrr...it sure looks cold where this cartoon character is paddling her kayak.

Keys

Here's how to draw a key in 3 steps:

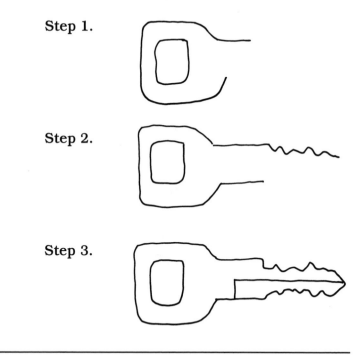

Step 1.

Step 2.

Step 3.

Overlap several drawings of keys and you'll have a whole lot of keys on your key chain.

Kicking

Draw a cartoon character with one leg up. Add the other leg.

Add a ball. Draw movement lines and an impact explosion.

Horses kick backwards.

Kites

Start by drawing a large diamond. Now draw a line from top to bottom and side to side.

Add a tail. Just draw lots of bow ties, like this:

Now all we need is a good breeze and we can go kite flying!

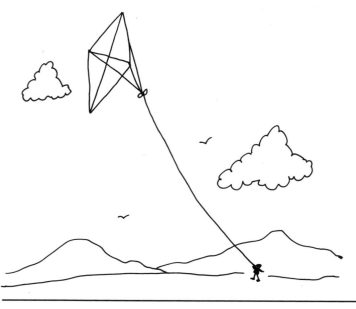

Laughter

When cartoon characters laugh, their eyes sometimes squinch up like this boy's eyes:

If cartoon characters laugh REALLY hard, sometimes their tongues stick out like this:

And if a cartoon character is laughing uncontrollably, he might roll around on the ground. I wonder what's so funny?

Leaks

This bucket is leaking. To draw a leak, draw lots of teardrop shapes coming from one spot.

Anything that holds liquids can leak...especially babies!

Leaves

Here's an easy way to draw a simple leaf. First, draw this shape:

Next, draw a line going down the middle of the leaf and add some veins.

Leaves come in lots of shapes and sizes.

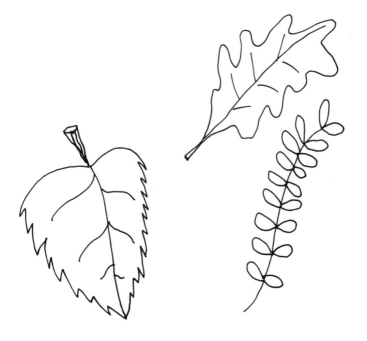

Litter

The trick to drawing litter is to draw lots of broken and bent things on the ground.

If the litter smells bad, draw some "stinky" lines
and some flies too.

Locks

To draw a lock, start by drawing a rectangle. Add
a circle in the middle. Now draw a small rectangle
inside the circle.

Next, draw a horseshoe shape on top of the
rectangle.

The lock on the opposite page uses a key. The lock below is a combination lock.

To draw a combination lock, draw some circles inside of each other then add some short lines around the edge of one of the circles.

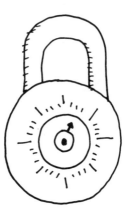

Logs

Start by drawing a cylinder. Add a small branch on top.

Now draw some circles on the end of the log.

Add some lines along the side of the log and draw a leaf on top.

I think this little guy is building something. What do you think it could be?

Magnets

Draw a horseshoe shape.

Darken the ends of the magnet. Add some lightning.

When you want to show someone being "pulled" towards something, you can draw the little lightning shapes. This guy is being pulled into an alien spaceship.

Maps

Draw a piece of paper. Don't make the edges too straight.

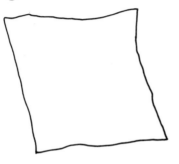

Add little pictures, a dotted line and an "X" to mark the location of the treasure.

Road maps can help you find your way, but once you unfold them, it's sure hard to get them to re-fold the right way.

Masks

Draw this shape:

Add this shape:

Draw some holes for eyes.

Decorate your mask with feathers, sparkles and jewels.

Meat

Draw a shape that looks like a lily pad.

Draw lines that go straight down from each curve. Add some lines along the bottom and you've drawn a nice, thick steak.

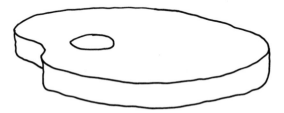

Turkey and chicken are called, "white meat."
Here's how to draw turkey or chicken on a platter.

Mountains

This is the way most people draw mountains. Not very interesting is it?

Instead, make your mountains uneven and give them several peaks.

Some mountains are round and smooth. That usually means they're very old.

Some mountains are flat on top. They're called "mesas."

Music

A musical note is simple to draw. Just draw an oval and a straight line. Now add a triangle and darken the shapes.

Look who's singing!

If the music is very loud, draw BIG notes. If the music is off-key, bend the notes. Like this...

Nails

Nails can be dots. Or circles with points.

Dots

Circles with points

If somebody has tried to build something and it's not very good, you can bend the lines on each nail.

Nests

Start by drawing a curved "X" shape.

Now, add some more curved "Xs."

Curve the bottom so it looks like a bowl.

You did it!

Draw a baby bird in a nest saying something funny to its mama.

What other funny thing could the baby bird say?

Nets

Begin by drawing a shape that looks like a ring. Add a handle.

Now draw the netting. Be sure to make the lines loose and wavy. Don't draw any straight lines when you draw the netting.

Even if you have a net, you have to be pretty fast to catch a butterfly. What else do people catch in nets?

Newspapers

Draw this shape:

Add pages.

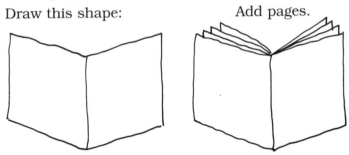

Now draw pictures of people and lots of squiggly lines for words.

If someone is reading a newspaper you might only be able to see that person's fingers and the top of his or her head.

Noses

Noses can be round, pointy, short, broad, or tiny.
Try drawing some of these noses.

Usually it's best to draw tiny noses on children.
Larger noses work best on adults.

Octopuses

Draw the top of the head, a smiley face and some eyes.

Add eight long, skinny arms.

Here's a riddle! What kind of sea creature will you see at the movies? *An ACTOR-pus!*

Odors

Here's one way to draw an odor in the air:
These hot, chewy cookies smell wonderful!

If you draw someone saying, "Sniff, sniff," that means he or she can smell the odor in the air.

SNIFF
SNIFF

Opossum

Draw a face and a head
that look like a mouse.

Add a round body and a long curvy tail.

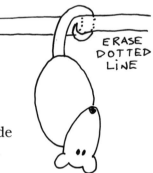

ERASE
DOTTED
LINE

Now turn your drawing upside
down and add a tree branch.

Opossums like to hang upside-down. Here's a mama opossum and her babies.

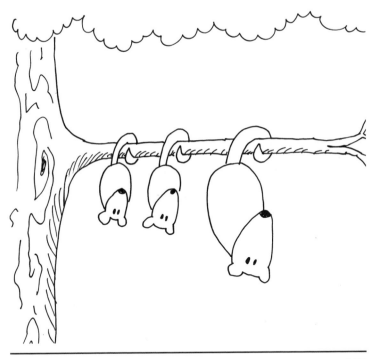

Ornaments

Draw a circle.
Add two rainbow shapes on the top.

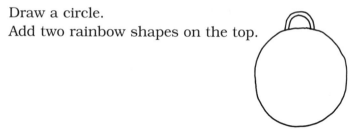

Draw repeating shapes on the side of your ornament.

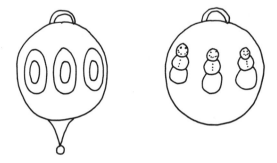

Draw a Christmas tree, and then add lots of different kinds of ornaments on the side.

Owls

Draw a tall rectangle.
Add pointy ears and big eyes.

Now draw some triangle toes, a triangle mouth
and two wings.

When owls get together, they ask the funniest questions.

Oysters

Draw this shape:

Add a curved line on the bottom.

Give your oyster some eyes.

Finish with some lines on the shell and some bubbles.

Doodle idea! Draw two oysters, draw something unusual on one of the oysters' shells then make one of the oysters say something funny.

Paint

Draw a shape that looks like snow on the roof.
Add a curved line.

Now draw a paint can. Don't forget to add a
handle.

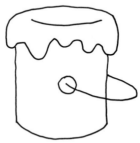

Try drawing the can lots of times and making the paint a different color each time.

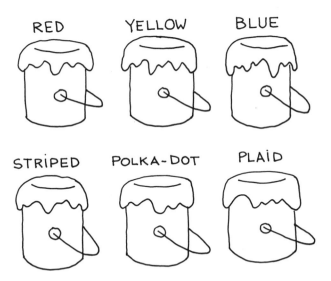

RED   YELLOW   BLUE

STRIPED   POLKA-DOT   PLAID

Pans

Draw this shape:

Add a handle.

Put something in the pan and add "heat" lines.

Draw someone cooking something really strange.

Paper

Here's how to draw a stack of paper.
Start with a diamond shape.

Add lots of lines on one side...

Add more lines on the other side.

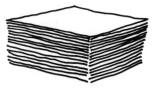

This poor teacher has too many papers to grade.
Whew!

Parachutes

Start by drawing a shape that
looks like the top of an umbrella.

Now draw a small character below
the umbrella shape.

Add lines from each point of the
umbrella to the character.

Some parachutes are shaped like rectangles.

Paths

To draw a path, draw two curvy lines that touch at the top. It's a little like drawing the number "3" twice.

Add bushes and trees along the sides of your
path.

Pedestals

Draw three rectangles. Like this:

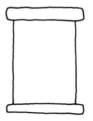

Add some of these shapes on the side of your pedestal.

It's not unusual to see a statue on top of a pedestal.

Queen

Draw a simple face, neck and body. Part the hair in the middle.

Add a crown and you've drawn Her Royal Majesty.

There are lots of different kinds of queens. There are queen bees, queen ants, and beauty queens. Try drawing some other kinds of "queens."

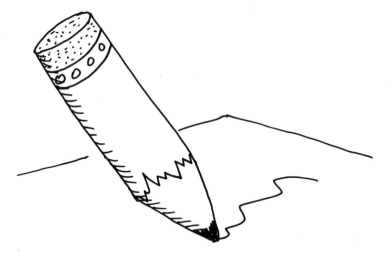

Questions

When cartoon characters have questions, they often look "up."

Lots of times they cover their mouths with one finger too.

Sometimes a cartoon character will scratch his or her head when the character has a question.

Rabbits

Start with a round head, a "Y-shaped" nose and some eyes.

Step 1.

Step 2.   Step 3.

Draw the same rabbit smaller several times and you'll have a mama rabbit with her bunnies.

Radios

Start by drawing this shape:

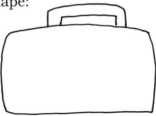

Add lots of squares and rectangles. Add an antenna too.

Do you get the feeling that we're about to hear some REALLY LOUD music?

Rafts

Draw a log.

Add circles and lines.

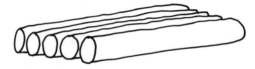

Tie the logs together with a rope.

Here's a little guy taking a ride down the river on his raft.

Robots

You can draw robots by "stacking" these shapes:

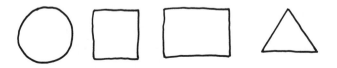

Here are a few combinations:

The trick to drawing cool robots is to draw lots of little shapes inside bigger shapes.

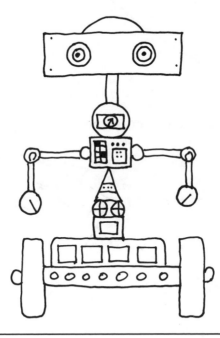

Rockets

Draw this:

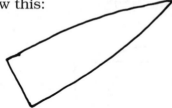

Add fins, windows and some rocket blast.

If you draw your rocket pointing up, it will look like it's taking off.

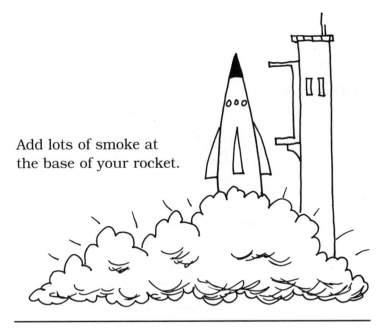

Add lots of smoke at the base of your rocket.

Rocks

Draw a big shape and a little shape next to it.

Add some shading.

To give your rocks a finishing touch, draw some grass nearby—and pebbles and dirt.

We usually see rocks in piles, so when you draw
rocks, draw LOTS of them. Make some big and
some little.

Sailboats

This is the kind of sailboat most people draw.

Let's draw something BIGGER!

First draw this shape:

Add big sails and some
windows on the side.

Draw a sailboat, add some water.

If you draw some smaller sailboats in the distance, you'll have a whole fleet of boats!

Scrolls

Draw a "backwards" S-shape:

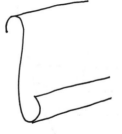

Add three straight lines:

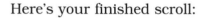

Here's your finished scroll:

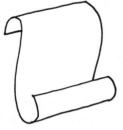

Add some "important sounding" words to your scroll.

Shading

Objects that have flat sides are shaded very dark
on the side that is away from the light.

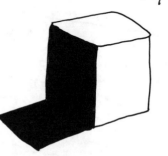

Objects that are rounded
have "softer" shading.

By looking at the shading in this drawing, where would you say the light is coming from?

Spiders

Spiders can be drawn with some very simple lines.
Draw a smiley face.

Add a body.

Now stick some legs on
the sides of the body.

What nursery rhyme do you think this cartoon is illustrating?

Little Miss Muffet.

What song is this cartoon illustrating?

"Itsy Bitsy Spider."

Tepees

Tepees are basically triangle shapes. Add bumps at the bottom and add a door too.

Draw some sticks on top.

Color in part of the inside of your tepee.

Draw a basic tepee then add lots of colorful designs.

Teeth

You can draw teeth that look like windows...

Or teeth that are round
on top and bottom.   Or weird teeth.

Sometimes goofy characters have just a couple of teeth showing.

Telephones

Draw this shape:

Add buttons and an antenna.

When somebody is holding a phone, you may not see much of the person's hand. You might only see the ends of the person's fingers.

Telescopes

Draw a tube shape.

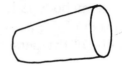

Add a smaller tube.

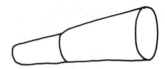

And one more tube and an eyepiece.

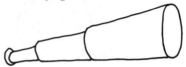

It's funny if you show the person's eye looking out of the end of the telescope.

Thermometers

Draw a rectangle. Add the basic thermometer shape.

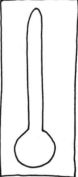

Add some numbers on the side.
Color in part of the thermometer.

The hotter it is, the more of the thermometer is colored in.

Ties

Here's an easy way to draw a man's necktie:

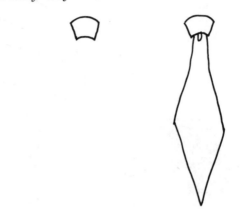

Bow ties start out as little squares.
Add "butterfly" wings.

Dad has a necktie. Junior has a bow tie.

Umbrellas

Draw this shape:

Now add a handle.

When you draw beach umbrellas, it's a good idea
to make them lean to one side a little.

Underground

First, draw some grass. Then add the hole in the ground.

Now draw some rocks and dirt around the hole.

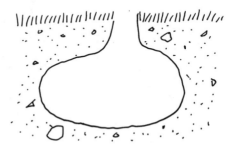

Draw a little critter living inside its underground house.

Vegetables

Here are some simple vegetables that you can draw:

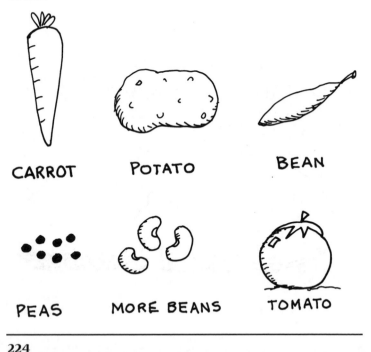

CARROT   POTATO   BEAN

PEAS   MORE BEANS   TOMATO

These are vegetable plants. Draw the same plant over and over in a row and you'll draw a vegetable garden!

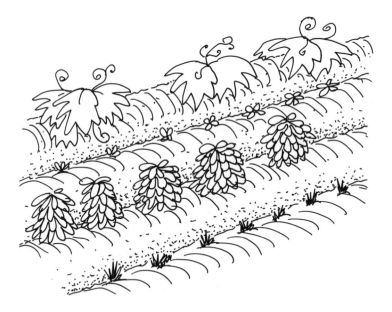

Veins

You can draw veins by making lots of squiggly "Y" shapes. Like this:

When someone has tired eyes you can see the veins in his or her eyes.

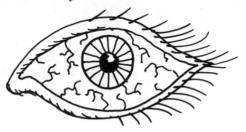

You can draw veins on an alien's brain too. Cool!

Vines

One way to draw vines is by starting with a heart-shaped leaf.

Draw more heart-shaped leaves.
Erase the lines where the leaves overlap.

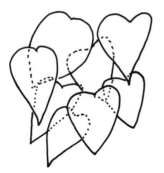

Add some curly cues.

You can draw vines on a fence or on the side of a house. You can also draw vines wrapped around a tree.

Volcanoes

To draw a volcano, begin with a shape that looks like snow on a roof...

Then add the mountain underneath...
And some smoke.

Draw a prehistoric scene with a volcano and some dinosaurs.

Walruses

Begin by drawing two eyes, a nose, and some
tusks.

Add a bumpy body...

Now draw some flippers
and some whiskers.

You can draw your walrus sunning on a beach or on a warm rock.

Watches

Draw two circles and add some arrows. . .

Now draw one end of the watchband. . .

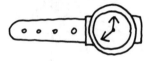

Then add the other end of the watchband.

When someone is wearing a watch, all you can see is the face of the watch and a little of the watchband. This cartoon character is looking at his watch. He looks worried, doesn't he? Maybe he's late.

Webs

Draw a circle, then add lots of smiley face lines.
Connect the smiley face lines
to the circle with straight lines.

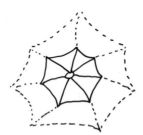

Keep adding more smiley
face lines and
connecting them
with straight lines.

The outer edges of the spider web are straight lines.

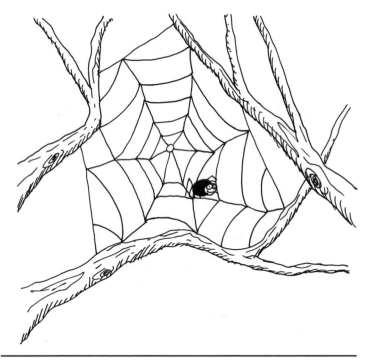

Whales

Draw this shape.

Add a mouth and an eye. The tail looks like a heart turned sideways.

If you draw a small whale next to a big whale, it looks like a mama whale with her calf.

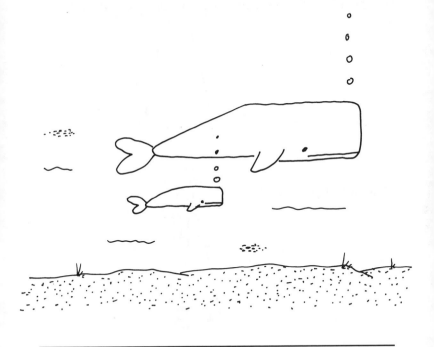

Windmills

Windmills look a little like beehives.
Draw a beehive shape with a door and windows.

Add a big propeller.

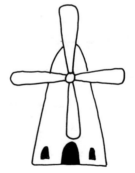

Here's a simple drawing of a tulip.

Draw lots of tulips and it will look like your windmill is in Holland.

Winks

Here's a wink.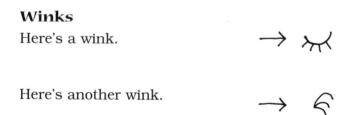

Here's another wink.

You can draw whichever wink you like best.

Sometimes when people wink, it makes other people spin around.

Woodpeckers

On a piece of paper, draw woodpecker number 1. On another piece of paper, draw woodpecker number 2. Try making both woodpeckers the same size.

Now, place your drawing of woodpecker 1 on top of woodpecker 2. Flip the top page and watch the action!

Wrenches

Draw two circles connected by two lines.

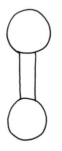

Inside each circle, draw a shape that looks like a little house. Erase the "floor" of the houses and PRESTO! You've drawn a wrench.

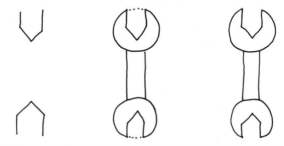

Whew! Even with a big wrench, this guy is having trouble.

Yawning

If you want to draw people yawning, be sure to include these elements:

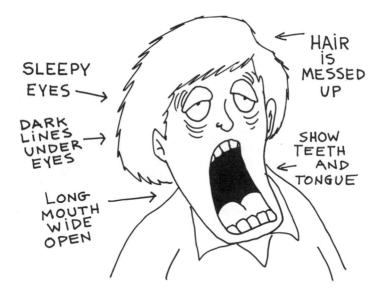

SLEEPY EYES →

HAIR IS MESSED UP ←

DARK LINES UNDER EYES →

SHOW TEETH AND TONGUE ←

LONG MOUTH WIDE OPEN →

It's even funnier if you bend the bottom of the mouth.

Zeppelins

Begin by drawing a long, skinny football shape.

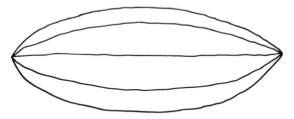

Add a fin on the top.
Then draw a rectangle and an egg-shape (motor)
on the bottom.

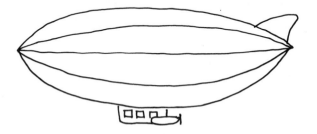

In World War II, blimps and zeppelins were used to spot submarines under the water.

Want to know more?

If you like to doodle, there are some great books that can help you develop your skills. Ask your librarian to show you where to find cartooning books on the shelves. You can also practice drawing the cartoons on the comics page of your local newspaper as well as the characters on cereal boxes and candy bar wrappers.

Your local bookstore probably has some good cartooning and doodling books too. Just remember that doodles are very simple cartoons. Look around and you'll find tons of little cartoons on things around your house.

There are lots of great cartooning and doodling web sites on the Internet, too. Just do a search on the words, "cartoons," "cartooning," "doodles," and "doodling." You'll probably find hundreds of places to go to learn about cartoons, doodles, and how to draw.

And finally, it's always a good idea to create your own original doodles. Look for simple objects around your house, school, and other places you go. Draw them as simply as possible; don't try to add a lot of detail.

Keep practicing and pretty soon you'll be a world-class doodler.

Good luck!

About the Author

Mike Artell is an award-winning children's book author, illustrator, television cartoonist, and conference speaker. Each year, Mike visits with more than 12,000 students at 50 schools across the country. During his school visits, Mike shows kids (and teachers!) how to think funny, write funny, and draw funny. For complete information about Mike's books and personal appearances, visit his web site: www.mikeartell.com

Index